D1090912

Falcons

by Ashley P. Watson Norris

Consultant:
Tanya Dewey, PhD
University of Michigan Museum of Zoology
Ann Arbor, Michigan

CAPSTONE PRESS
a capstone imprint

First Facts is published by Capstone Press,
1710 Roe Crest Drive, North Mankato, Minnesota 56003.
www.capstonepub.com

Library of Congress Cataloging-in-Publication Data
Norris, Ashley P. Watson.
 Falcons / by Ashley P. Watson Norris.
   p. cm.—(First facts. Birds)
 Includes bibliographical references and index.
 Summary: "Discusses falcons, including their physical features, habitat, range, and life
cycle"—Provided by publisher.
 ISBN 978-1-4296-8606-8 (library binding)
 ISBN 978-1-62065-249-7 (ebook PDF)
 1. Falcons—Juvenile literature. I. Title.
QL696.F34N67 2013
598.9'6—dc23
                              2012002160

Editorial Credits:
Lori Shores, editor; Juliette Peters, designer; Kathy McColley, production specialist

Photo Credits:
Corbis: Galen Rowell, 10-11, Papilio/Bryan Knox, 17; Dreamstime: Neal Cooper, 6, 14,
Robmckay, 20; Getty Images: Photo Researchers/Anthony Mercieca, 15; Newscom: Danita
Delimont Photography/Steve Kazlowski, 19, WLP/Douglas Graham, 9; Shutterstock:
EcoPrint, 5, Hedrus, 13, mlorenz, 12, Pavel Mikoska, 1, Sue Robinson, 21, Thomas Barrat,
cover

Artistic Effects
Shutterstock: ethylalkohol, Pavel K, pinare

Essential content terms are **bold** and are defined at the bottom of the page where they
first appear.

Printed in the United States of America in North Mankato, Minnesota.

042012   006682CGF12

Table of Contents

Small and Mighty

Falcons are like fighter jets of the animal world. They turn, twist, and spin while flying at high-speed. Their flying skills make them mighty hunters.

Falcons can be many sizes. Most falcons have a 3 foot (0.9 meter) **wingspan**. Gyrfalcons are the largest. They weigh up to 4 pounds (1.8 kilograms). American Kestrel falcons weigh only 3.5 to 5.5 ounces (99 to 156 grams.)

wingspan—the distance between the outer tips of a bird's wings

lanner falcon

eyes

beak

wings

talons

Razor-Sharp

Falcons are built for hunting. They have strong wings for fast flying. Powerful eyesight helps them spot **prey** far away. Falcons use sharp **talons** to snatch small animals and carry them away. Their razor-sharp beaks tear their meal into bite-size pieces.

Falcon Fact!

Falcons see three to four times better than people do.

prey—an animal hunted by another animal for food

talon—a large, sharp claw

Where Falcons Fly

Nearly 50 kinds of falcons live all over the world. They live on every **continent** except Antarctica.

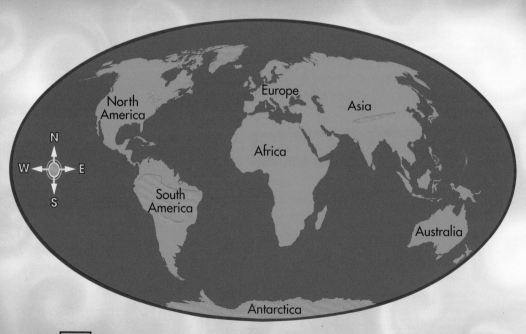

North America

Europe

Asia

Africa

South America

Australia

Antarctica

N
W E
S

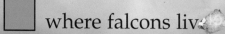 where falcons live

peregrine falcon

Falcons live in all sorts of weather. Gyrfalcons live in cold, northern areas. Prairie falcons live in hot desert areas. Peregrine falcons can **adapt** to live almost anywhere. Some falcons even live in cities.

continent—one of the seven large land masses of Earth

adapt—to change behavior to fit in a new situation

9

Skyscraping Nests

Falcons nest on high places, such as cliffs, ledges, and tall buildings. These nests are called scrapes. Falcons make them out of rocks, pebbles, and sticks. Falcons use the same scrapes year after year if there is enough food nearby.

Falcon Fact!

Kestrel falcons sometimes make nests in tree holes.

prairie falcons

Falcons in Flight

Falcons don't **soar** like other hunting birds. They flap their wings quickly as they fly. To spot a falcon, watch for quick wing beats.

American kestrel

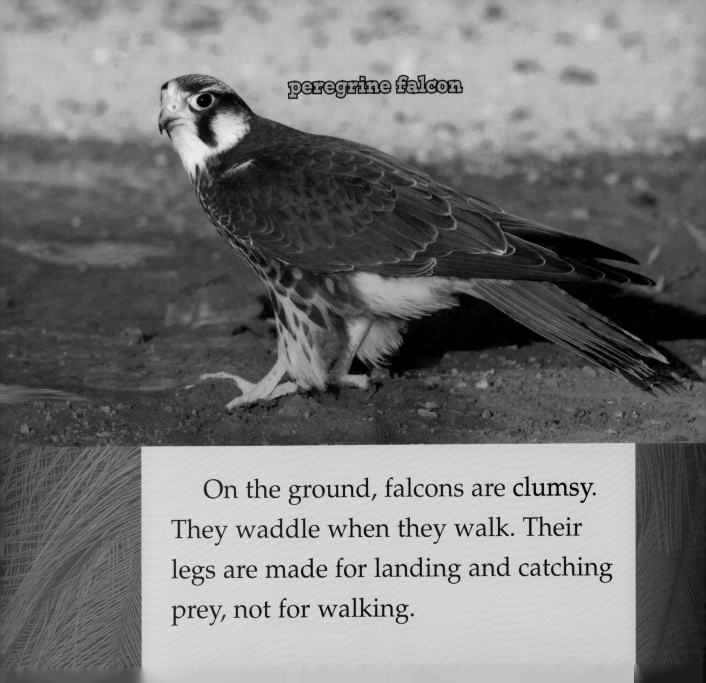

peregrine falcon

On the ground, falcons are **clumsy**. They waddle when they walk. Their legs are made for landing and catching prey, not for walking.

Carryout

Falcons look for small birds and animals from high in the sky. Some falcons fly while they hunt. Others watch from a high lookout.

red-necked falcon

When falcons spot prey, they tuck their wings and dive. They hit the animal with their feet first. Then they grab it with their talons and carry it away.

Falcon Families

Female falcons lay one to seven eggs in spring. The **mating pair** takes turns warming the eggs. The female moves the eggs around so they don't get too warm or cold.

Falcon Fact!

Peregrine falcons mate for life. Unless one of the mating pair is killed, they will not take other partners.

Life Cycle of a Falcon

Newborn: Falcon chicks have a thick layer of fluffy white feathers.

chicks

Young: At three weeks old, falcons are 10 times their size at hatching.

Adult: Falcons can live up to 15 years.

Falcon chicks hatch in about 30 days. In another month, they are **fledglings** with flying feathers. They flap their wings to get ready to fly. Parent falcons provide food while the fledglings learn to hunt.

Falcon Fact!

A young falcon that hops around its nest is called an eyas (AHY-uhs).

fledgling—a young bird that is learning to fly

young gyrfalcons

Falconry

People have been using trained falcons to hunt for years. The falcon stands on a falconer's arm. When the falconer throws his or her arm upward, the falcon chases after prey.

gyrfalcon

Amazing but True!

peregrine falcon

Peregrine falcons are the fastest animals in the world. They can dive faster than 200 miles (322 kilometers) per hour. Small falcons can fly up to 45 miles (72 km) per hour. Larger falcons can reach 62 miles (100 km) per hour.

Glossary

adapt (uh-DAPT)—to change behavior to fit in a new situation

clumsy (KLUM-zee)—careless and awkward in the way something moves or behaves

continent (KON-tuh-nuhnt)—one of the seven large land masses of Earth

fledgling (FLEJ-ling)—a young bird that is learning to fly

mating pair (MATE-ing PAIR)—a male and female animal that join together to produce young

prey (PRAY)—an animal hunted by another animal for food

soar (SOR)—to fly without flapping wings

talon (TAL-uhn)—a large, sharp claw

wingspan (WING-span)—the distance between the outer tips of a bird's wings

Read More

Haywood, Karen. *Hawks and Falcons.* Endangered! New York: Marshall Cavendish Benchmark, 2011.

Lundgren, Julie K. *Falcons.* Raptors. Vero Beach, Fla.: Rourke Pub., 2010.

Lunis, Natalie. *Peregrine Falcon: Dive, Dive, Dive!* Blink of an Eye. Superfast Animals! New York: Bearport Pub., 2011.

Internet Sites

FactHound offers a safe, fun way to find Internet sites related to this book. All of the sites on FactHound have been researched by our staff.

Here's all you do:

Visit *www.facthound.com*

Type in this code: 9781429686068

Super-cool stuff!

Check out projects, games and lots more at
www.capstonekids.com

Index